Brands We Know

Nintendo

By Sara Green

WITHDRAWN

Bellwether Media • Minneapolis, MN

Jump into the cockpit and take flight with Pilot books. Your journey will take you on high-energy adventures as you learn about all that is wild, weird, fascinating, and fun!

This edition first published in 2016 by Bellwether Media, Inc.

No part of this publication may be reproduced in whole or in part without written permission of the publisher.
For information regarding permission, write to Bellwether Media, Inc.,
Attention: Permissions Department,
5357 Penn Avenue South, Minneapolis, MN 55419.

Library of Congress Cataloging-in-Publication Data

Green, Sara, 1964-
 Nintendo / by Sara Green.
    pages cm. -- (Pilot: Brands We Know)
 Summary: "Engaging images accompany information about Nintendo.
The combination of high-interest subject matter and narrative text is
intended for students in grades 3 through 7"-- Provided by publisher.
 Audience: Age: 7-13.
 Includes bibliographical references and index.
 ISBN 978-1-62617-350-7 (hardcover : alk. paper)
1. Nintendo video games--Juvenile literature. I. Title.
GV1469.32.G74 2016
794.8--dc23
                    2015033108

Printed in the United States of America, North Mankato, MN.

Nintendo®

Table of Contents

What Is Nintendo?

Homework and chores are finished. Now it is time for Nintendo! Two friends are excited to play *New Super Mario Bros. Wii*. Each works a remote. One friend plays Mario. The other is Luigi. Soon, their characters are jumping on platforms, collecting coins, and scrambling over obstacles. Sometimes the friends work together to beat the level, but not always. Suddenly, Mario throws Luigi into a lava pit! Luigi escapes, but for how long?

Nintendo is a Japanese electronics company. It is best known for its video games and **consoles**. It also makes playing cards and other toys. The company **headquarters** is in Kyoto, Japan. Nintendo is one of the most successful video game companies in the world. Characters such as Mario and Pikachu have become world favorites. They have helped Nintendo become one of the world's most well-known **brands**.

By the Numbers

worth more than
$22 billion
in 2015

nearly
700 million
Nintendo consoles
and handhelds sold
worldwide

more than
200
games that
feature Mario

more than
10.5 million
amiibo figurines sold
as of 2015

more than
5,200
employees

more than
4 billion
video games sold
worldwide

more than
700
Pokémon species
in 2015

**Nintendo
headquarters**

From Cards to Video Games

In 1889, a man named Fusajiro Yamauchi started Nintendo in Kyoto, Japan. The company made small, thick playing cards called *hanafuda*. These colorful cards were made by hand from tree bark. Later, the company also made the standard 52-card decks that are popular in western countries. Over time, Nintendo became the largest card-making company in Japan.

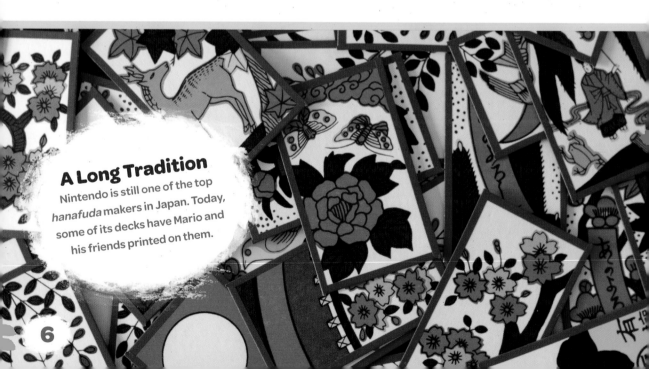

A Long Tradition
Nintendo is still one of the top *hanafuda* makers in Japan. Today, some of its decks have Mario and his friends printed on them.

Hiroshi Yamauchi

In 1949, Fusajiro's grandson, Hiroshi Yamauchi, became president of Nintendo. Hiroshi was young, but he had big ideas. He got permission to make Nintendo cards printed with images of Walt Disney characters. The cards were very successful. In 1959, Nintendo sold 600,000 packs! Hiroshi also expanded the company into other areas. Nintendo ran a food company and a taxi service. It also made toys and games. Hiroshi decided Nintendo worked best as a toy company. In time, he shifted the company's focus to electronic games. This decision would change video games forever.

In the 1970s, Nintendo began making coin-operated **arcade** machines. Its first game, released in 1975, was called *EVR Race*. This horse racing game had some success. However, it was an arcade game called *Donkey Kong* that made Nintendo famous worldwide. *Donkey Kong* was the first **platform video game**. Released in 1981, it introduced Jumpman, later known as Mario. Jumpman's goal was to save his girlfriend from a barrel-throwing ape. *Donkey Kong* quickly became the top-selling arcade game in the world.

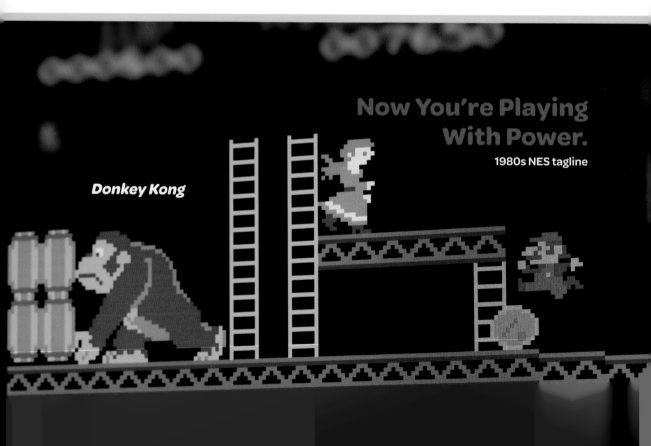

Donkey Kong

Now You're Playing With Power.

1980s NES tagline

.... *Super Mario Bros.*

**Nintendo
Entertainment
System** ....

In 1985, Nintendo introduced the Nintendo Entertainment System (NES) to the United States. This console and controller allowed people to play video games at home. A favorite was *Super Mario Bros.*, created by *Donkey Kong* designer Shigeru Miyamoto. In it, Mario runs and jumps through the **quirky** Mushroom Kingdom. The side-scrolling platforms and **intuitive** controls drew many people into the video game world. *Super Mario Bros.* became one of the most successful video games of all time. Mario soon became Nintendo's **mascot**!

....

Shigeru Miyamoto

Naming a Game
Miyamoto wanted to name *Donkey Kong* after its stubborn gorilla. He saw in the dictionary that *donkey* could mean stubborn. *Kong* is named after the gorilla called King Kong.

A few years later, Nintendo introduced Game Boy. Nintendo had made portable games before with the Game & Watch. But each handheld device was only programmed for one game. The new Game Boy used **cartridges**. These allowed players to play many games using the same device. At first, they only played in black and white. One of Game Boy's first games was called *Tetris*. To play, people put falling puzzle pieces into correct spots. People loved this simple game. *Tetris* helped Nintendo sell millions of Game Boys. Later, a new Game Boy that played games on a color screen pushed sales even higher. By 2000, Nintendo had sold more than 100 million Game Boy handhelds.

Game Boy

Game Boy Color

Game Boy cartridges

Pokémon for N64

Pocket Monster
The Pokémon Mini is Nintendo's smallest handheld. It is about the size of a playing card.

Pokémon for Game Boy

One Game Boy game sparked a worldwide craze. In 1996, a **role-playing** game called *Pokémon* was introduced in Japan. It arrived in the United States in 1998. People could catch, train, and trade creatures called Pocket Monsters, or Pokémon. Children loved these adorable, colorful characters. Over time, Pokémon became the second-best selling video game series ever, after Mario.

During this time, the company also continued to improve its larger consoles. The Super Nintendo Entertainment System (SNES) came out in the early 1990s. It was faster and could play more complicated games. Its game library introduced favorites such as *Super Mario World* and *Super Mario Kart*. The game *Donkey Kong Country* made history. Its **graphics** were among the first to appear 3D.

Now You're Playing With Power. Super Power.

1990s SNES tagline

Super Nintendo Entertainment System

Super Mario 64

GoldenEye 007

Nintendo 64

The Legend of Zelda: Ocarina of Time

The Nintendo 64 (N64) was introduced in 1996. It offered fewer games than earlier consoles. However, many became huge hits. *GoldenEye 007* introduced many people to **first-person shooter** games. It helped make the **genre** widely popular. *Super Mario 64* moved platform games from scrolling 2D levels to rich 3D worlds. *The Legend of Zelda: Ocarina of Time* wowed players with its detailed world and gameplay. It is called one of the best video games of all time.

Magic Flute

An ocarina is a real type of flute that appears in some of the Zelda games. The character Link plays tunes on an ocarina to solve puzzles, travel through time, or even change night to day.

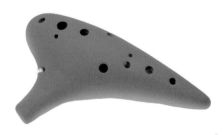

13

Games for Today and Tomorrow

In 2006, Nintendo introduced the **innovative** Wii gaming system. Players direct games with a slim, wireless remote. A **sensor** picks up the motion of the remote. It causes players' movements to control things onscreen. Balls fly across soccer fields or land deep in tennis courts. Some games, such as *Skate It,* use a special balance board for extra motion technology. Many favorite Wii games star Mario, Link, and other classic Nintendo characters. People play as characters called Miis for some games. They can create Miis to look like any person they want!

Wii
balance board

Wii would like to play
2000s Wii tagline

In 2012, Nintendo's Wii U system took the Wii technology even further. Some games allow up to eight people to engage in non-stop action. The special GamePad controller features a touch screen, speakers, a camera, and more. People can play games right on the GamePad. They can even watch TV or walk out of the room while still playing on the Wii U!

Popular Plastic Figures

Figurines called amiibo make Wii U and 3DS play even more fun. Players tap their amiibo against the game pads. Then the characters come to life on screen.

Nintendo is always working to make its games and systems more fun. Its latest handheld device, the New 3DS XL, is better than ever. People can play games in 3D without glasses. They can also stream videos, snap photos, and record videos in 3D. Meanwhile, the company is hard at work creating new games and products. In 2015, Nintendo announced a new console, code-named NX. It is top secret. Most people believe it will work at home and on the road. Some think it will be the first home console since the N64 to use cartridges. Nobody knows for sure what Nintendo will release next!

While people wait for the new console, they keep busy playing *Super Mario Maker*, *Splatoon*, and other popular games. Nintendo games for smartphones will add to the fun. Nintendo plans to release games for mobile devices in the coming years. Playing Nintendo games on the go will be easier than ever. With so many game choices and ways to play, everyone can enjoy Nintendo!

Nintendo World Championships

In 2015, Nintendo hosted the Nintendo World Championships in the United States. People played games such as *Splatoon*, *Mario Kart 8*, and *The Legend of Zelda* for prizes.

Top-Selling Nintendo Games of All Time

Name	Year Released	Genre	Games Sold
Wii Sports	2006	Sports	82+ million
Super Mario Bros.	1985	Platform	40+ million
Mario Kart Wii	2008	Racing	36+ million
Tetris (for Game Boy)	1989	Puzzle	35+ million
Wii Sports Resort	2009	Sports	32+ million
Pokémon (Green/Red/Blue)	1996 (Japan)	Role-playing	31+ million
New Super Mario Bros.	2006	Platform	30+ million
New Super Mario Bros. Wii	2009	Platform	29+ million
Duck Hunt	1984 (Japan)	Light gun shooter	28+ million
Wii Play	2007	Party	28+ million
Nintendogs	2005	Digital Pet	23+ million
Mario Kart DS	2005	Racing	23+ million

Bringing Smiles to People

Nintendo brings fun to people in tough situations. The company supports Starlight Children's **Foundation**. This organization is dedicated to helping sick children and their families. Through the foundation, Nintendo donates Fun Centers to hospitals around the world. These mobile units each have a Nintendo console, a screen, and a DVD player. They roll right up to hospital beds or anywhere the kids want to play. Fun Centers brighten days and bring families close together in difficult times. Today, Nintendo has helped put more than 8,500 Fun Centers in hospitals around the world.

Nintendo has also raised money for Operation Smiles. This program helps children who were born with mouth **deformities**. Medical teams travel around the world to repair the children's mouths. The surgeries improve children's health and quality of life. Through its products and community service, Nintendo brings smiles to people across the globe every day.

**Starlight
Fun Center**

19

Nintendo Timeline

1889
Fusajiro Yamauchi starts
a playing card company
in Kyoto, Japan, called
Nintendo Koppai

1959
Nintendo starts selling
cards printed with Walt
Disney characters

1983
Mario Bros. is introduced

1975
The arcade game *EVR Race*
is introduced

1981
Donkey Kong
is released

1963
The company's name
changes to Nintendo, Co., Ltd

1985
The Nintendo Entertainment System
is launched in the United States and
Super Mario Bros. is released

1989
Game Boy is introduced
in the United States

1998
*The Legend of Zelda: Ocarina
of Time* and *Pokémon
Red/Blue* are released in
the United States

2006
The Wii is introduced

1994
Donkey Kong Country
is released

2012
The Wii U is released

1996
Nintendo 64 is launched

2009
Game Boy is inducted into
the National Toy
Hall of Fame

1987
The Legend of Zelda and
Metroid are introduced in
the United States

1991
The Super Nintendo
Entertainment System is
launched in the United States

2015
Nintendo announces
the NX project

Glossary

arcade—an indoor area containing coin-operated games

brands—categories of products all made by the same company

cartridges—small electronic devices that contain video game software; cartridges are put into consoles to play video games.

consoles—electronic devices for playing video games on a television screen

deformities—conditions in which body parts do not have normal or expected shapes

first-person shooter—a type of video game in which the player shoots enemies and other targets; in these games, players view the action through the eyes of the characters they are controlling.

foundation—an institution that provides funds to charitable organizations

genre—a specific type of game or story

graphics—art such as illustrations or designs

headquarters—a company's main office

innovative—introducing new ideas and methods

intuitive—to know something immediately without having to think about it

mascot—an animal or object used as a symbol by a group or company

platform video game—a type of game in which characters jump on platforms to get to new places

quirky—unusual in an interesting way

role-playing—games in which people pretend to be specific characters

sensor—a mechanical device that responds to information such as pressure, light, or motion

To Learn More

AT THE LIBRARY

Kaplan, Arie. *The Epic Evolution of Video Games.* Minneapolis, Minn.: Lerner Publications Company, 2014.

Maltman, Thomas James. *The Electrifying, Action-Packed, Unusual History of Video Games.* Mankato, Minn.: Capstone Press, 2011.

Sutherland, Adam. *The Story of Nintendo.* New York, N.Y.: Rosen Pub. Group, 2012.

ON THE WEB

Learning more about Nintendo is as easy as 1, 2, 3.

1. Go to www.factsurfer.com.

2. Enter "Nintendo" into the search box.

3. Click the "Surf" button and you will see a list of related web sites.

With factsurfer.com, finding more information is just a click away.

Index